QUEEN AND STRANGER

QUEEN AND STRANGER

TRAVVIS LARGENT
CHAPBOOK SERIES

No. 3

By

Sara Jeanine Smith

USPOCO BOOKS
Pensacola, FL

for Naomi and Ada

USPOCO BOOKS, a non-profit publisher, is a division of **us poetry company**.

All rights reserved under International and Pan-American Copyright Conventions. Published in the United States by USPOCO BOOKS, Pensacola, FL.

uspocobooks@gmail.com

QUEEN AND STRANGER
Copyright © 2019 by Sara Jeanine Smith

ISBN 978-0983306290
Library of Congress Control Number:

FIRST EDITION

CONTENTS

Walking with My Daughter	1
Dog Days	5
Grandma	9
Brother	11
March	15
That Spring	17
My Daughter Knows the Night	19
I Never Wait for the Muse	21
Rattletrap	23
Profligate	25
Lost	27
To Carve the Way Forward	29
The Crossing	31
Composition	33
Shell	35
As My Daughter Learns the Words	37
Aftermath	39
Tongues and Feet	43

my shadow
the cross
that one day will bear me away.

>   *T. Crunk*

Walking with My Daughter
    after Thoreau

I recall myself as shameless crosser of property lines,
seeker of climbing trees, importer of muck, forger of paths
that did not circle back until sundown.
Then, I remember myself as almost-mother,
plodding purposefully to summon labor,
willing you to arrive. After you crashed
your way into the daylight, my tiny, squinting spectacle,
I walked with you in my arms, hungry for sleep.
This is what it means to give place to darkness,
the not knowing:
my best walks have led nowhere quite tangible.
My best prayers have flitted among my footsteps,
a fleeting litany of atmospheres unknown.

Taller now, you dart down the trail in the January light
that here is short-lived, and sharper for being far away
in this place where seasons sprint out of succession,
summer coming always soon.
And you too, are all out of order,
making playgrounds of crumbled clay,
crunching deer moss, chasing lizards,
learning that sap is the blood of pines,
and cypresses have knees.
I pray that you can stay a little while this way,
and not forget that border life where even the winter sun
shines brighter when splintered by the shade of magnolias,
and cooled in the tangled refuge of Florida scrub.

To decide for the swamp, those shadow remnants
of springs unfurling from aquifer to gulf,
is to speak a world for wildness, and so much more so
here where swamp once reigned and still creeps, unruly,
into the margins of the subdivisions.
Scribble some of yourself into the margins,
find that backwater
that can't be filled or drained, divided or sold—
and part of you will stay a child of the mist,
plunking each foot nearer to the good,
rambling toward that holy land.

Dog Days

I never saw the Siberian huskies
next door to my grandmother's back yard.
Corralled in their thirty-foot run, they paced
their portion of the West Palm suburb.
Each summer, I saw only their silhouettes,
filtered through the cracks in the picket fence,
a zoetrope clicking through splintered motions.

I remember the broad faces of hibiscus blooms,
the banyan tree's fingers pressing the ground,
toads squatting in gutter buckets and the hiss
of the screen door spring and those humid hours
when stillness made my childhood stall.

But mostly, I recall the sliced outline
of dogs bred to bound through snow.
I could feel their fur tremble in the Arctic wind
and the tug of the sled over tundra.

They should have been all teeth and tongue and tail,
playful snarl and sleepy sigh.
But they were only shadow and bellow,
the most mournful yodeled howl I ever heard.

Their baying broke hot molecules of air,
air that would have glittered over snowdrifts
but here hung heavy over cracked patio

and the Norfolk pine in the front yard
standing guard like a Christmas monolith,
its shadow stretching with the afternoon.

Grandma

When you were born, your mother was so old
there was no milk left for you. Likely
it was long since drunk up by your brothers.
There was a cow, but the milk made you vomit
and break out in hives. So the old doc (God bless him)
said to fry up bacon real crisp, grind it
into a powder, mix it with water.
And that is what you drank until someone found a goat.
That creature saved your life. But they said
that for a whole year, you never stopped bleating.
Sometimes, you could still feel the grit of that bacon
in your throat, or maybe it was the Oklahoma dust,
staining your lungs.

Brother

I was six and you were three
when the old shed caught fire.
Our mother, in a flurry of maternal fear,
told us to sit like stones
on the brown and orange couch
and wait for further instruction.
You were more still than I had ever seen you
since the day you were born.

You had always tried to fidget and fuss your way out
of this world, into your own, but here you were,
silent as pondwater. You did exactly as I told you,
as though the entire world was engulfed and ending.
I was transfixed by your small face,
so serious, looking straight ahead
into an inferno that children couldn't see.

For a moment, we were Gretel and Hansel in a dark wood,
searching for breadcrumbs,
straining to hear the shouts
of parents and neighbors, any distant yell
that meant they weren't dead yet.

Our mother would laugh years later
about the hose my father told her to fetch,
which had already burnt in half. But no one was laughing
until the fire was out.

Now that we are older, I want to tell you
that it is we who are outside fighting the flames.
I want to yell at you to soak down your clothes,
tie a rag over your face, and get moving.
I want to shake you and say that no adults
will come to check on us, return to reassure us,
wiping sweat and soot from their foreheads.

I am afraid
I don't know you very well now,
but I am still sitting beside you.
We are staring straight ahead, our faces ashen.

We have never left that couch.

March

It was March when I first knew of you, March also
when I first felt your life was a lie.

You were an ode to all things off-kilter, not quite right,
and every mother became a reminder
of that task to untell what was told,
undo what I was working up to.

If you were a dream, I've been waking up from you
for seven years, relishing that last bit of sleep
when I believed you were true.

If you were a song, you'd be some half-remembered
string of chords, a fragment of a melody I can't quite play.

If you were a star, you'd be the one shining
from farthest away;
I wouldn't be quite sure you were there,
but I'd wish on you
and for you
anyway.

That Spring

when rain dumped all night
until it seeped up through our cracked foundation,
spurting from between the bathroom tiles,
bubbling bizarrely from the grout,
squeaking through the numb light of 2 a.m.,
creeping to fill half the house with an inch of water,
a puddle that lingered, then receded
as the sun emerged,

as though God had changed His mind.

My Daughter Knows the Night

is a dark wheel, and she has a stick
to mark each thought that circles her bed.
Her music is not of the spheres,
but of spokes interrupted.

She tells me that God won't let her sleep,
but that when He does,
she needs someone there to listen to her dreams.

I Never Wait for the Muse

I could treat each day like food for a poem,
like fuel for a poem,
like each drop from the coffeemaker
is a new iteration of my inspiration,
each measured repetition
an alliteration linking form to feeling,
like this track I'm jogging around is a new
node of meaning, each jagged stride a song
from which my genius seeps,
each pant a pantoum, each lap
an ode to all that runs this tight ship.

I could whip up rhymes like scrambled eggs
and sling them on your plate
and make you clean it.
I could find transcendence
in the sizzle of bacon grease;
I could click carseat buckles in iambs;
I could bathe babies and each splash
would be a stanza; my enjambments
would drain your expectations
like bathwater, and then I'd shower you
with similes. At dinner
I could feed you some line
of bullshit with your meatloaf
and you would even be thinking
I was cutting through it—

Rattletrap

Some symbols clatter past me in a rickety wagon,
lickety-split down a washboard road.
I still shake when it is over.

A few glide by, inexplicably
guided by a gleaming notion
I didn't know had caught me.

I'm startled by the noise I make starting:
the ignition switch shrieks when I turn it,
and even if I get this ramshackle show on the road,
I have a sneaking suspicion that putting on the brakes
will send the whole jalopy careening into the ditch
where its carcass will rust silently for decades.

I've spent quite a clunking
chunk of my life by the side of this highway,
my sneakers crunching busted bottles and scorched wild-
flowers, waiting to hitch a ride with some well-intentioned
fool in the driver's seat asking me over and over

what's wrong, why don't you say something

Profligate

Accept this baptism of ditchwater,
receive this communion of moldy crust,
and confess that the finding is in the losing,
for you hold tightest to the things that are slipping—

at the precipice, you suddenly realize
the sumptuous thrill of squander:
the slickness of palm sweat,
the shaking heft of this moment,
this body, this blood,
poised to betray.

Somewhere in your heart, a trash fire burns.
You are ravenous, a mutt roaming
through endless alleys,
sniffing each rotted remnant.

Yet these things flung aside
have a way of finding you in the dark,
like a discarded God
who whispers beside you in the pit,

I am here

Lost

I know I haven't written to you in a while,
and I no longer think of you every day
as I once did, driving to work, my hands hardening
around the steering wheel. But you are still with me
because even a lack carves out its own space,
an ache in this body that couldn't carry you long enough.

I see you in the smile
of the daughter whose cells
would never have knitted together
if yours hadn't fallen apart.
I find you in the faces of those
I could have easily called friends
but something got in the way,
didn't pan out as planned.
I hear your voice in the sentences
I have been stringing together
in my head forever,
but can't bring myself to say.

I love you the same as I have loved so many others
I have never known, and I still want you,
same as when I thought I would get to meet you someday,
same as the way I want words
to mean more than they do.

To Carve the Way Forward

I keep crumbling into the rifts that call me
        to unearth more of myself
                this gift that gathers and trembles
                      shifts and tumbles

but now in the night I will unfurl before you
        in the springtime I will fall all around you
            and I keep returning to the places
                I have been given without asking

Every still thing has within it
        the mention of movement
               like when I fold myself into the dark
                      my ear curls around silence

I hear the world tilting in its sleep
        plates drifting to nest in new resting
                rivulets molding the contours of rocks
                      predicting the shape of morning

The Crossing

I don't know where you are,
but perhaps I could first try
to cross this river, my skirt ballooning,
then soaking up the metallic water
as I stumble to the other side.

My flesh will tighten against the cold,
my soggy steps gaining speed as the light fades,
until I find you, finally, in whatever field you huddle,
or perhaps sprawl. I will startle when I see
whatever shape you make
in the gray dusk, the stubble
of cornstalks pricking your skin.

I could carry you, though my arms would ache
like branches grown brittle in winter.
A bitter tremor would pulse through me.
I might drop you.

The ways I could find you are infinite.
The ways I could gather you up
are yet to be determined. I can't plan, only conjure
vague shapes to blot the blackness behind my eyes,
scrambling to find whatever it is
I could become for you.

Composition

What if you could summon forth a gumption
from that segment of yourself that no one sees?
What if you could muster that inner army necessary
to tackle all things full tilt?
What if you could write yourself into being
the person required for the moment,
and what if each note
was as deliberate
as a song composing itself,
gathering to a crescendo,
like ants escaping a flood,
climbing and clinging
into a breathing, seething
monument to urgency?

And what if fragments
forced to coalesce
only scatter later,
ants retreating as the water recedes,
or spent dogwood blossoms
crumbling into shards
of light—

And what if you compose yourself
only to fall apart,
as though instead of a fortress,
you are really its gate,

flung wide open?

Shell

If I show up as a shell of a person,
there is less pressure to perform.

I can fill my crustaceous carapace
with whatever fragments flow my way:
with both whims and wisdom,
the detritus of this dying world.

I'll be the best bottom feeder
you've ever seen.
I can molt when things get old
or don't go my way,
and my soft-shelled self will be so new,
you won't even know how to eat me.

Or, I could admit that I am built
to inhabit a shell that is not even mine,
curling into a hardened home
left by some other soft species
who once needed it.

As My Daughter Learns the Words

she scales the jagged cliffs of consonants,
skims the plateaus of vowels,
rappels down the edges of letters to the valleys
of the blankness between,
and every line becomes a scatter of echoes:
shapes become sounds, and sounds form images
that bounce back to her, familiar and
yet wholly Other,
as she maps new territory, this country
in which she is both queen and stranger.

Aftermath

It is easy to forget
that everything shattered
was already broken
before the storm blew through,
already had within it
a penchant for flying apart.

You have always been sweating
alone in your soggy living room,
listening to the drone
of your neighbor's generator.
You have always been burning
your last drop of gas while in line to get more.
The milk in your fridge has always been souring,
just a little more slowly.
You have always been searching
for a signal, waiting for the grid to be restored,
the tower to resurrect.

You have always been combing the rubble
for something of value,
wondering when help will arrive
as you realize you weren't prepared
and never will be.
You have always been clutching a shotgun,
guarding your ruins from looters.

It is only after the air is quiet

you know that the trees have been waiting
their whole lives for wind to uproot them,
as though the prophets were right
when they said there'd be reckoning,
as though God had howled through the rain,
He'd sooner blow your rotten house down
than let you back in it.

Tongues and Feet

When I was nine and unbaptized,
I found God in a five-gallon bucket.
It was neon orange, marked with flaking labels
about its former contents, like unreadable runes.
The neighbor woman with the vast bosom
hauled it and me to the country church.

A velvet painting of a waterfall hung above the altar,
and women filed in to wash and be washed.
In faded and threadbare dresses, they dared
proclaim to God, *I am here*, dared
to shake the air with voices wavering
between a sob and a shout, dared
to use the prayer language left at Babel,
left at Pentecost, left at the foot of the cross, left at my feet,
white and bare, submerged in an orange bucket,
scrubbed by a dozen hands,
dried with heavy hair uncoiled
like the splendor of sound over silence.

In my gut, I felt the roiling moans,
the syllables that stabbed the sanctuary
like fever-flashes. I wanted to sip
the secret grace they drank,
to mimic in my pagan way
the sweet and terrifying uptick of octaves
I was unworthy of.

I never learned their language, though I still hear it
like a stranger's blood rushing through my veins,
water erupting from sleeping springs.

I never went back to that church, but I am still holy.
I am still always
at the edge of weeping.

ACKNOWLEDGMENTS

Acknowledgement is made to the following publications for poems that originally appeared in them:

Beyond the Quiet Desperation, booklet for Artel Gallery "Walking with My Daughter"

Weatherbeaten Literature "Dog Days"

Mothers Always Write "March," "As My Daughter Learns the Words"

www.ingramcontent.com/pod-product-compliance
Lightning Source LLC
Chambersburg PA
CBHW070458050426
42449CB00012B/3036